BASKETBALL

By Mark Littleton

ZondervanPublishingHouse
Grand Rapids, Michigan

A Division of HarperCollins*Publishers*

Basketball
Copyright © 1995 by Mark Littleton

Requests for information should be addressed to:
  Zondervan Publishing House
  Grand Rapids, Michigan 49530

Library of Congress Cataloging-in-Publication Data

Littleton, Mark R., 1950–
        Basketball / Mark Littleton.
            p. cm.—(Sports heroes)
        Includes bibliographical references.
        ISBN: 0–310–49561-X (softcover)
        1. Basketball players—United States—Biography—Juvenile
    literature. 2. Basketball players—United States—Religious life—
    Juvenile literature. [1. Basketball players. 2. Christian life.]
    I. Title. II. Series: Littleton, Mark R., 1950–Sports heroes.
    GV884.A1L58 1995
    796.357'092'2–dc20   94–44873
    [B]   CIP

                                                                      AC

Edited by Tom Raabe
Interior design by Joe Vriend

Printed in the United States of America

      96 97 98 99 00 / ❖ DC / 10 9 8 7 6 5 4

To Jon, Scott, Jeff,
and all the boys in afternoon hoops.
Oh, for those days again.

Contents

The Razzle-Dazzle Sport of Basketball

Basketball hasn't always gotten the respect it gets today. Until the sixties, it was a slow-paced, methodical game that didn't draw crowds. Today, it's a razzle-dazzle, fast-paced, fast-break sport that keeps fans on their feet.

In this book, you will meet some of the razzle-dazzle players of the past and present. What's more, Jesus has come to be the most important person in each of their lives.

So come along and meet some of the greats of a sport that we all enjoy. Hear their testimonies, learn their best moves, root for them. And above all, remember that they're just guys who seek first God's kingdom. And that's something we can all excel in.

Mark Littleton
February, 1995

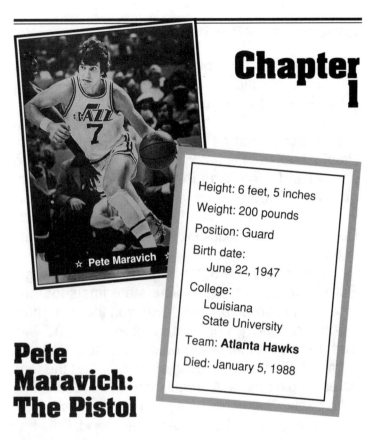

Chapter 1

⭐ Pete Maravich ⭐

Height: 6 feet, 5 inches
Weight: 200 pounds
Position: Guard
Birth date:
    June 22, 1947
College:
    Louisiana
    State University
Team: **Atlanta Hawks**
Died: January 5, 1988

Pete Maravich: The Pistol

Pete Maravich grew up in a unique situation. His father, Press, worked as head basketball coach for Clemson University in Clemson, South Carolina. Pete's father was a basketball genius who used his two sons, Pete and Pete's older brother, Ronnie, to try out his latest schemes. And Pete tried them all. Behind-the-back passes, through-the-legs passes, up, down, and all-around shots. Pete became a human library of basketball tricks, and he brought them onto the court for Daniel High School where he started playing guard as early as eighth grade. Pete became the playmaker of the team.

Pete also learned to shoot. In fact, it was as an eighth grader that he gained the nickname "Pistol Pete" because his shot looked like he was drawing a pistol and firing. With Pete's shooting prowess at guard and brother Ronnie's abilities at strong forward, along with several other talented players, Daniel High School quickly became the team to beat in the area.

In the last game of the regular season, though, Pete suffered a setback. The state finals loomed around the corner, and whoever won this last game would probably go on to the state finals and win. With Pete's brother being double-teamed, Pete put on a dribbling and shooting show that had the fans screaming for more. As regulation time ended, it was a tie game. The game was pushed into overtime.

Close to the end of the overtime period, Pete had the ball. His team was down by one. He dribbled down, weaving in and out, looking for the shot. Some in the crowd shouted, "Shoot! Shoot!" as others counted down, "Ten, nine, eight . . ."

Still, Pete kept looking. No one was open, or if they were he didn't fling the pass. Finally, with only two seconds on the clock, he fired. The ball had a beautiful backspin. If Daniel High scored, they would almost certainly win state.

But the ball struck the rim and bounced out as the buzzer sounded. Pete's team had lost. Pete himself was devastated. His family encouraged him, though, and gradually he came out of the losing funk. He decided that the next year would be the year, and he looked forward to it.

During the next two years Pete added five inches of growth onto his skinny, slight body. He became much more aggressive. His sophomore year, he averaged 21 points a game.

That summer, Pete's father transferred from Clemson to North Carolina State to be an assistant coach. Pete moved on to Needham-Broughton High School for his junior year. They'd had a losing season the year before, but were in the most powerful and prominent conference in the state. Pete had grown to just under six feet tall, but weighed a slight 130 pounds. Opponents could easily pummel him physically on the court if he was not careful. He led his team to a 19–4 record that year, one of the best in the state. However, in the semifinals of the championships, they lost by 1 point on a controversial call. It was one more loss Pete didn't know how to deal with. Why couldn't he win the big ones?

His senior year, Pete grew another few inches, rounding off at six-four. He averaged 32 points a game and was recognized as the team's leader. However, he was the only returning starter that year and had to lead a green team. It seemed that when he was hot the team was on, and when he cooled off, so did they. Too much responsibility fell on his shoulders, and Pete spent a lot of time feeling depressed and broken after a loss. They ended the season with plenty of losses too, racking up an 8–13 record.

Pete had had a good two years at Needham-Broughton, though. He scored 1,185 points, averaging 32 points a game. Thirteen times he scored over 30 points in a game and six times over 40. In the North Carolina All-Star Game, Pete broke a record with 47 points.

He was still a skinny and slight kid, though, and his father knew he couldn't stand up to the physical play of college ball. The family decided to send Pete to Edwards Military Academy, a college-prep school, where Pete could incubate a little. He had been pouring all his energies into basketball, and his academics had slipped. Pete needed to pull up his grades, learn some discipline, and prepare himself for big-college ball.

In one game at Edwards, Pete pumped in 50 points and made headlines. Then Edwards went up against a rival, the North Carolina State freshman team, and the newspapers hyped it as Maravich against Maravich, Pete against his dad. Even though his father didn't coach the freshman basketball team, it made for a nice rivalry. Pete scored 33 points and led Edwards to a 91–57 blowout.

During that year, college offers started pouring in for Pete from around the country. At the same time, Pete's father got an offer to be head coach at Louisiana State University, a school not known for powerful basketball teams. LSU wanted to rebuild, and they thought Press Maravich could be their man. Pete himself was stunned. Why would his father leave a great school like NC State for LSU?

Pete had no idea what was coming. Pete wanted to play for West Virginia, a well-known basketball school, but his father wanted Pete to play for him at LSU. Pete's father cornered him at the Pittsburgh airport where Pete was flying out to do a clinic. He wanted Pete to sign something—a "grant-in-aid" for a player—which meant a scholarship for Pete and a sure berth on the team.

Pete balked. He didn't want to go to LSU. They had nothing there for him except his father. And he didn't know whether that was enough.

Father and son stood off against one another in that lonely airport:

Pete argued, "No way! You gotta be kiddin' me, Dad. LSU? That's a football school! Dad, you wanted me to play ball for West Virginia, and that's what I'm gonna do."

15

His Dad shouted back, "You're coming with me."

"No!"

The tense display went on and on. Two angry Serbs fighting for supremacy in the relationship. Finally, his father said, "Sign the paper, son . . . or don't ever come home again!"

Pete had never seen his father like this. He knew he couldn't fight him anymore. He signed the form.[1]

Pete's years at LSU would prove to be the most productive and winning time of Pete's life. And he had the opportunity to learn more about basketball from the very man he revered and loved, his own father.

Why did his father want Pete to play for him? Press Maravich believed basketball could be an exciting, thrilling game when players used some of the razzle-dazzle methods he believed in. Tricks. Showmanship. A little spectacle was what was needed—and Pete was the perfect person to pull it off. He was a flashy player, knew hordes of tricks, could spin a ball on his fingertips for hours, and knew how to use it all on the court. College basketball up to that point (the late 1960s) tended to be a plodding, slow-moving game. In fact, many schools hardly had programs in place. Stands certainly weren't filled. The big sport was still football.

But Pete's father wanted to change that, and with his son he thought he had the perfect vehicle. Thus, the 1966–67 season looked hopeful. Pete would play on the freshman team while his father got the varsity ready for his coming the following year (freshmen were ineligible to play varsity back then).

That year, the LSU varsity performed miserably. The Tigers went 3–23. Attendance was off. Things looked dismal.

But something else was happening. In the "Cow Palace" (where LSU played its basketball games), the freshmen would play prior to the varsity game. And the "Baby Bengals" were something else, led by none other than Pistol Pete Maravich. He passed behind his back, through his legs, and over his shoulders. The slowed-down, sluggish game of basketball turned into a high-velocity, fast-break, all-out, catch-as-catch-can spectacle. Suddenly, tickets for the freshman Tigers' games were the hottest items on the block. People who showed up for the freshmen would leave afterward, uninterested in seeing the varsity perform.

It was showtime for Pete, who was averaging 43 points a game. Six times he went over 50 points, and he had a high of 66 one night against an independent Baton Rouge team. The Baby Bengals racked up seventeen straight wins going into the last game of the year, against Tennessee. With LSU down 75–73 in the final seconds, Pete got fouled and went

17

to the line for a one-and-one. If he sank both free throws, the game would be tied.

Pete sank the first one easily. As the crowd simmered down to silence, he lofted the second ball. It rolled around the rim and spurted out. Time ran out, and the Tigers lost their last game of the season. Once again, Pete tasted the bitter fruit of loss when a towering victory was only a shot away. Why did it always happen to him this way? He still had not learned to cope with loss, and the pain grated on him. He felt empty and demoralized inside, even though to many he was a hero.

During Pete's first year on varsity, the 1967–68 season, Pete and his father became household names as records fell to the onslaught of Pete's jump shot. That year he scored 1,138 points, averaging 43.8 points a game, the highest in collegiate history. One night against the Crimson Tide of Alabama, Pete had his highest scoring game while on varsity. With the clock ticking down to zero, Pete crossed the half-court line and whisked the ball aloft. It fell through the hoop for his 58th and 59th points of the evening. No one had ever made so many points in a single game in the Southeastern Conference.

By season's end, Pete had smashed four national, sixteen SEC, and nine LSU records. He made the all-SEC team and was voted MVP of the league. United Press International and the Associated Press put Pete on their all-American teams. The

United States Basketball Coaches Association also named Pete, the lone sophomore, to their all-American team that included Wes Unseld, Elvin Hayes, Don May, and Lew Alcindor (who later changed his name to Kareem Abdul-Jabbar).

That summer, Pete went to the Olympic tryouts in Albuquerque, New Mexico. His father warned him that selection to the team was somewhat skewed and political. Pete might not make it because he was just a sophomore and a star individual rather than a "team" player, at least not the type of the team player the Olympics required.

Pete played in three games, a total of about two minutes in each. He wasn't selected to the Olympic team. It was one more defeat for him.

But it didn't slow Pete down. During the Christmas holidays of Pete's junior year, LSU played in the Oklahoma City All-College Tournament. There they faced some of the great teams in the country, including nationally ranked Wyoming, the favorite Oklahoma City University team, and a Duquesne team that was number nine in the country. LSU upset all three. The highlight came in the third game against Duquesne. With fifteen seconds left, an LSU teammate sank two free throws, then Pete got fouled and iced the game with two more free throws. They went back to Louisiana as heroes.

His junior year, Pete broke more scoring records, including Bob Pettit's LSU career record of 1,972 points and Elvin Hayes' two-season NCAA record of 2,097 points.

In the last game of the season, against Georgia, with LSU leading, Pete ran down the final minute of the second overtime to seven seconds, then dribbled to the corner of center court and with three seconds left, hooked a shot toward the basket. It touched nothing but net. The crowd went wild, and Pete was lifted high above the floor by the *Georgia* cheer-leaders! Pete scored 1,148 points that year, hitting .444 from the field and .746 from the free-throw line. And he still had a year to go.

More records toppled during Pete's senior year. One was Oscar Robertson's three-year scoring total of 2,973 points, perhaps the greatest record on the NCAA books. He broke it on January 31, 1970. Pete needed only 39 points to break the record and already had 25 at the half. With 7:50 left in the second half, Pete dribbled down court, sank a brisk fifteen-footer, and tied Robertson's record. The crowd was half-crazed with the fever pitch of the moment.

Then for the next three minutes, Pete failed to score. On his fifth attempt to break the record, Pete drove and, from 23 feet out, leaped. Fully extended, he flicked his wrist. The ball sailed perfectly through the hoop. The crowd seemed to explode around him and suddenly the floor was filled with fans, all screaming, all grabbing for a piece of Pete Maravich.

All Pete himself wanted was to finish the game. He ended the night with 53 points and 12 assists.

LSU finished the year with a 20–8 record and went to the National Invitation Tournament (NIT) with high hopes. Pete went into the tournament holding 25 records. Eleven of them were national, and plenty of players he would oppose were gunning for him.

In LSU's first game Pete didn't play well, and the Georgetown Hoyas' defense held him to 20 points. But LSU won, 83–82. They also won the next game and advanced to the semifinals against Marquette, the tourney favorite. Pete was still not playing well, though, and he felt it. When friends came over with some beer, he made one of the biggest mistakes of his life: he got drunk and stayed up half the night. He played the next day, the most important game of his career, with a very bad hangover.

It was no contest against Marquette. The stronger team defeated Pete's Tigers, 101–79. Pete scored a measly 20 points. When it was all over, Pete was devastated. Once more his own failures had taken the ultimate success from his hands. Was he born for failure? Would he ever reach that elusive championship?

That year, though, Pete set a career scoring record that has not yet been bettered—3,667 points—even though he only played three years and

83 games (44.2 points per game, career). During his senior year, he led the nation in scoring with an average of 44.5 per game, and had the most games with 50 or more points, both that year (10) and in his college career (28).

Out of college, Pete signed the first million-dollar contract awarded a basketball player. He went with the Atlanta Hawks. His three seasons there, though, were unspectacular. Pete's style of play did not seem to fit in with the conservative Hawks. Many of the players seemed to resent the money and media time Pete commanded because of his celebrity status. He could not seem to break into their inner circle. Still, he placed among the top ten scorers for two of those years, finishing fifth in 1972–73 with 26.1 points per game and second in 1973–74 with 27.7 points per game.

He was traded after three years to the New Orleans Jazz (who later became the Utah Jazz). The Jazz were building a team from scratch, and it was difficult for Pete. He spent several uneventful seasons there and failed to win the championship he had dreamed of for years. Nonetheless, he remained in the top ten scorers, coming in third in 1975–76 with an average of 25.9 points per game and finally, in 1976–77, winning the league scoring title with 31.1 points per game.

He married his college sweetheart, Jackie, but still a darkness dragged at Pete's heart. He could not seem to find any happiness. His days were filled with depression, anger, and hatred toward various enemies.

In 1980 he found himself a member of the Boston Celtics. In a preseason game, Pete scored 38 points, but in the locker room someone told him the coaches were saying he had a long way to go before he would be a true Celtic.

Pete had suffered through several injury-heavy seasons, and he was fed up. He felt empty inside. His mother had committed suicide several years earlier. In some ways, he felt his life was over. What he didn't know was that he was on a collision course with Someone who would soon become the most important person in his life.

Pete walked away from basketball and went into seclusion. For two years, he stumbled around as a recluse, refusing to talk to the press, struggling to get his balance in a world gone awry. One night in November 1982 he lay in bed, unable to sleep. He felt burned up and burned out about nearly everything in his life. He kept thinking about all the rebellion he had toward God. The drinking. The anger in his family life. The many moments of failure on both the basketball court and with his father and mother. He felt as if his mind were crushing him.

At 5:40 A.M. he cried out to God. "I've cursed you and spit on you. I've mocked you and used your name in vain. I've kicked, punched, and laughed at you. Oh, God, can you forgive me, can you forgive me? Please, save me, please. I've had it with this life of mine. I've had it with all the world's answers for happiness. All of it, the money, fame, and things have left me so empty."[2]

He lay there listening to the deafening silence, wondering what might happen. Suddenly, a voice seemed to speak right out of the darkness. "Be strong. Lift thine own heart."

That was all. But Pete was so stunned he woke his wife and asked her if she'd heard it. She hadn't, and promptly fell back to sleep. Pete lay there and continued his prayer, "Jesus Christ, forgive me of my sin. I believe with all my heart that you died for me and rose from the grave so I would have eternal life. Make me the person you want me to be."[3]

For the first time in many years, Pete felt the void that had settled on him disappear. From that moment, his life was never to be the same.

Over the next few years, Pete came out of seclusion and began conducting basketball clinics with a spiritual emphasis.

Not much later in his Christian life, Pete felt he had to do something he'd avoided for years: apologize to his father for getting drunk the night before his miserable performance in the last game of the NIT. He went to his father and told him the story. His father tried to laugh it off, but Pete was serious. "No,

Dad, I'm serious. I will not leave this room until this is right between us."

Very quietly, Mr. Maravich forgave his son. An enormous burden lifted off Pete's shoulders.[4]

Several years later, Pete led his father to the Lord, and his dad also got involved in the clinics after his conversion. It was father and son again, the marvelous Maraviches doing their basketball thing!

On December 14, 1985, the Utah Jazz retired Pete's number seven in a stirring ceremony in Salt Lake City. Pete was never more honored.

Then on May 5, 1987, he was inducted into the Basketball Hall of Fame. It was a fitting high point to his startling career.

Pete died of heart failure in January 1988 at the age of 40. He had just published an autobiography and was planning to be interviewed by Dr. James Dobson on "Focus on the Family." It was an early and tragic end to a great career. But his impact will never be forgotten.

---

1. Pete Maravich and Darrel Campbell, *Pistol Pete: Heir to a Dream* (Nashville: Nelson, 1987), 96.
2. Maravich and Campbell, 192.
3. Maravich and Campbell, 193.
4. Maravich and Campbell, 206–7.

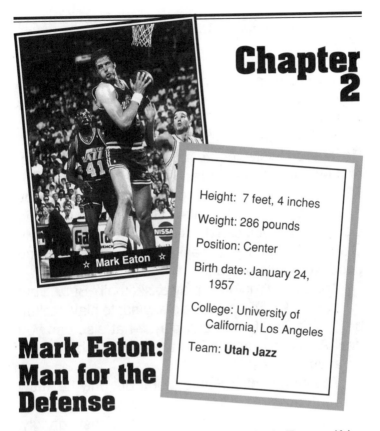

Chapter 2

Height: 7 feet, 4 inches

Weight: 286 pounds

Position: Center

Birth date: January 24, 1957

College: University of California, Los Angeles

Team: **Utah Jazz**

☆ Mark Eaton ☆

Mark Eaton: Man for the Defense

There's not an ounce of fat on Mark Eaton. If he were a middle linebacker, you'd be scared. But his sport is basketball, and he's a center for the Utah Jazz.

No small wonder. At seven-four, he has two feet or so on most of us. Even the Jolly Green Giant takes notice of this guy.

Mark Eaton did not come naturally to basketball. In fact, in high school he shied away from it, even though he was on the varsity. His coaches didn't know what to do with him. He sat on the bench, playing rarely. He didn't know any of the moves—he wasn't taught them.

So Mark decided to become an auto mechanic. He labored twelve hours a day working on engines, brakes, and front ends. He was making about $20,000 dollars a year, and he was basically happy except for the comments: "Hey there, up in the clouds!" "I bet you can dunk it!" "Yo! You up there! Mr. Giant!" "You must play basketball! Even if you're no good, you gotta be good."

And then: "You don't play basketball? But . . . but . . . but . . . ?" "You must be crazy not to play basketball!" "I mean, if you don't play, what else can you do?" As if a guy seven feet tall shouldn't be able to do anything else!

The comments irritated Mark. But only he knew the *real* cause of his irritation: He wasn't any good at basketball! He'd tried, but he was clumsy, gangly, slow. He wasn't like those quick and sly forwards and guards who danced around him for easy-as-pie layups. They almost laughed at him.

Who cares about basketball anyway? Mark thought. *There are other things in life besides that!*

Mark didn't figure that one of his customers, named Tom Lubin, would also be a basketball coach at Cypress Junior College, a two-year school in Phoenix. Tom took one look and knew Mark had to be a winner. At seven feet four, how could he not be? So Tom asked him point-blank, "Have you ever considered bas—"

"No," Mark interjected. He wasn't interested.

Tom kept after him. "Just give me one hour. That's all I ask. To show you some moves. See if you can do it." Tom knew he could sure use a seven-foot-four-inch guy on his team at Cypress.

So finally Mark relented, to get the guy off his back. It was only a couple of hours of working out. It might even be fun.

To his surprise, Tom showed Mark some "big-man moves" that were simple and easy to perform. Mark was amazed. He'd never learned any of these moves: the hook across the lane, the turnaround bank shot, the drop step. And he was introduced to defense. He found out that one of the center's main jobs was defense: blocking shots, keeping forwards and guards from driving down the lane, standing in the way.

Defense soon became Mark Eaton's main game. So in 1978 at the age of 21, Mark enrolled at Cypress Junior College. That year, he led his team to a 34–2 record. They made it to the Junior College state semifinals. Mark was so good at defense that he attracted the attention of some scouts and coaches in the NBA and was drafted in the fifth round by the Phoenix Suns. The team managers didn't want Mark to quit college, so it was kind of a "let's see what happens" situation. If Mark continued as he was, he would be prime material for the pros.

The next year, Cypress went 31–5 and won the state championship. Mark averaged 14 points a game and had over 600 rebounds in his two seasons with Cypress. He was playing well on offense, but defense was really his strength. At the same time, Mark was working nights as a car salesman. But he was very committed to school and basketball. He wanted a degree, and he wanted to play. To his excitement, he won a scholarship to UCLA, one of the best-known and most-watched teams in the United States. Maybe basketball really was his sport!

At UCLA, though, he had the same problem he'd had in high school—the coaches didn't seem to know what to do with him. UCLA was a down time for Mark. He played an average of only 3.6 minutes a game. In fact, he played more in his first two games in the pros than he did during his whole senior year at UCLA. The team didn't even take him on their last road trip. He felt discouraged, but he kept working. He believed he had some defensive gifts, and he hoped they could be useful in his future.

Frank Layden, head coach of the Utah Jazz, was watching Mark. He thought the kid had potential, and he knew exactly what to do with him if the Jazz drafted him. Frank persuaded his managers to at least take a look at Mark on videotape. Though Mark had excelled at Cypress, the games were not taped, so he had to find something good from his days at UCLA. It was hard, but finally he put together a short—"very short," he says today—video of himself on the court for UCLA.

The Jazz liked what they saw. They drafted Mark in the fourth round. Frank Layden made some promises to Mark, but Mark had heard promises before: in high school and at UCLA. In both places, he rode the bench. Years later, Layden would tell reporters, "Eaton did not come into the NBA with a lot of God-given talents. Most players were all-Americans in high school and college, and everyone paid them all sorts of attention. Mark never had that, so he came in hungry."[1]

Mark was hungry enough to work hard and do his best. He was the first person at the arena on practice days and the last to leave. He worked on his defensive moves most of all. He put in the time, and the coaches worked with him.

Mark's chance arrived in 1982, his rookie season. The Jazz became strapped for money and needed to make some cash moves, so they traded away Danny

Schayes, their first-string center. Mark was shoved into the starting spot. Mark says, "That was a big step for me. When Frank gave me the starting job, everything changed. All of a sudden, I had an opportunity that I hadn't anticipated. I determined to work even harder and maintain that job."[2]

Mark still wasn't a natural, except at defense. And there he worked harder than anyone. In fact, he became the "Big Man on the Block," as *Sports Illustrated* called him in an article on him in May 1986. That year, Utah won the Midwest Division with a 51–31 record. They were the top defensive team in the league, and Mark led the league in blocks. Behind Mark's powerful blocking and alley watching, the Jazz gave up only 99.7 points a game and held their opponents to a .434 shooting percentage, the second-best record ever behind the Milwaukee Bucks' .425 in the 1973–74 season.

Mark has a ninety-inch arm spread and wears size seventeen shoes. Seattle forward Xavier McDaniel said at that time, "He blocks up the middle like a tree."[3]

Mark's teammate Karl Malone said, "You think of defense, you think of the Jazz. You think of why, you think of Mark."[4]

Mark said he sees himself "clogging things up, messing up plays" in the middle. He just stands there, not jumping too much, both feet firmly planted on the ground, and then "eats them alive." In the

1984–85 season, Mark swatted down 456 shots and had at least one "rejection" in 84 consecutive games. That record still stands. He led the league four times in the eighties, with 4.28 blocked shots a game in 1984, 5.56 in 1985, 4.06 in 1987, and 3.71 in 1988. His 5.56 blocked shots per game in 1985 is an NBA single-season record (his 4.61 average in 1986, while second to Manute Bol that year, is the fourth-best single-season mark). He also holds the NBA record for the highest average blocked shots in a career at 3.68 per game (minimum of 400 games). In 1985 and 1989 he was selected as the NBA Defensive Player of the Year, and he has been named to the NBA all-defensive team three times. Only he and Kareem Abdul-Jabbar have logged over 3,000 blocked shots in their careers, and Mark is homing in on Kareem's record.

Some people are especially surprised at Mark's Christian testimony. Sometimes people think big guys are too "tough" or "macho" to embrace the teachings and person of Jesus. Gentle, mild, and humble, Jesus does not seem to represent the hard-driving, elbow-piercing, physical play of pro basketball. But Mark does not flinch at telling people of his professed faith.

He grew up in a churchgoing family. His six-foot-nine-inch dad and six-foot-one-inch mom always put a lot of stock in faith and tradition. Mark and his dad spent a lot of time in Mark's younger years in Boy Scouts.

As far as Christianity goes, Mark felt for a long time that he'd missed something. He called it "the missing link." He wasn't sure what that missing link was until, as a sixteen-year-old, he attended a church retreat with his youth group. He had grown up in a church that believed you were saved if you were baptized. But on this retreat, Mark ran into a young man from another church who told him about having a close relationship with the Lord. A personal relationship. Like friends.

Mark was amazed. He realized the personal relationship with God was the missing link he hadn't yet accounted for. He says, "It was kind of like a lightbulb went off there. . . . So I made a commitment to Jesus Christ."[5]

In an article for *Sports Spectrum* magazine, explained,

> It was not like fireworks. Instead, it was basically just an understanding on my part that I need to make a further commitment to God. It was a personal relationship with Him through Jesus Christ that I needed. I knew there was more to the Christian life than I was receiving. So I sat down and prayed with this guy that I would start a personal relationship with the Lord. I made a commitment to Him. From then on, I felt like I had a new understanding, and I guess I had a different

goal structure. It was like I woke up and discovered that there was more to life than I was getting. From that point, I tried to attend more Christian meetings, like a Bible club that met once a week.[6]

Mark has gone on to develop a robust, loyal faith in the Lord to lead him through everything. "To this point today," he says, "I've trusted the Lord with all major decisions I've had to make. Any times of crisis I've had to go through, even making the decision from being an auto mechanic to going to school, which was very traumatic for me. I was a good auto mechanic, and I was making a pretty good living at it. I wondered, *Am I supposed to walk away from this? Start over from scratch at something I'm not very good at?*"[7]

His wife, Marcie, and he have two children that they're raising in basketball and in the faith. His son, now in kindergarten, even attends some of the games and watches his dad. Mark says,

God has been a big part of my life and my family's life. We've relied on Him to guide our lives in every facet that's come about—whether it be a career change or sickness or where are we going to be next year. The best part of the whole thing is the fact that once I've given the decision to the Lord to make, I don't worry about it. That's one thing I've always been good at. I don't get too stressed out about decisions. I just say, Lord, help me with this. I'm going to give it to You—like that verse that says, don't worry about anything. The whole basis of my life is that I don't get stressed about things that I don't have control over.[8]

The Jazz team is quite close. Thurl Bailey, the co-captain, is also a brother in Christ and he and Mark are best friends. Mark feels strongly that teamwork and a love for Christ are good ingredients in building a powerful pro basketball team. He says, "I think that being a Christian is a definite help when it comes to dedication and working hard on improving yourself. As a humble servant, I think I look at myself in the same terms. I'm never satisfied with my perfor-mance. I've never stopped working hard."[9]

That kind of hard work has shown up in Mark's performance on the court and off. He is a gentleman, a dedicated husband and dad, and a respected teammate. Mark is most proud of his record 456 blocks in 1984–85. In fact, for those readers who might wonder what advice he'd give for defense, lis-ten to this:

> To be a good blocker, you have to understand what your role is on the team defensively. If you are the back one, you are the final line of defense. It's your job to shut down the middle. I basically look at the paint as my area. And anyone who comes in my area, whether it be a guard or a cen-ter, I feel it's my responsibility to stop him.

In that process, I get my body in front of him early and make him make a decision—whether he's going to shoot or whether he's going to pass.

The hardest part to learn about shot blocking for me was keeping my feet on the floor. This is a real key for young people, because you want to jump on every head fake and knock the ball into the fourth row. Well, what you're trying to do is stop that player from scoring. So, get over there in front of him, keep your feet, and don't go for the head fake. It's amazing what players will do when you don't go for their head fakes. They just lose control. They don't know how to react to that, and they'll take an off-balance shot or a bad shot, or they'll throw the ball away.[10]

That defensive posture is so effective that Mark's teammates pile on the praises. John Stockton, Utah's point guard during Mark's high-blocking seasons, said, "He makes people so nervous they don't have time to look for an open man. So if you stay in the play, even though you may have been beaten, there's a good chance the pass will be thrown to you."[11] Another Jazz guard during Mark's blocking heyday, Darrell Griffith, said, "If there was a stat for 'Just for being there,' Mark would be a 10 every night."[12]

None of that goes to Mark's head. He continues to be a hard player on the basketball court and a steady player in the court of the King. In fact, in the last year he has gotten involved with a company that puts on youth programs through AWANA, a Christian youth organization for churches. He participated in a basketball camp that included not only basketball, but life-style skills he wished he'd had as a kid. Mark wants to continue that kind of work once he leaves the NBA.

Mark has also been instrumental in bringing the basketball chapel program to the Utah Jazz. Mark was attending a church in Salt Lake City whose pastor sometimes put on chapels for the minor-league baseball team in town. He persuaded that pastor— Jerry Lewis (not the comedian)—to get a similar program going for the basketball players. After consulting with Frank Layden, they began. Today, the Utah Jazz have one of the strongest chapel programs in pro basketball.

Another thing Mark enjoys is hunting and fishing. In fact, he's had several encounters with grizzly bears! Taking fishing jaunts in Alaska, he's crossed turf with a few of those big bears where they like to fish. He says they know the best fishing spots too, so it's a little bit of a problem. But if he leaves the bears alone, they leave him alone.

All in all, Mark considers himself a defensive player. He still only averages 6 to 7 points a game. But he forces the other team to make mistakes, throw away the ball, and eat their own shots. And that's what wins ball games.

1. David Branon, *Slam Dunk* (Chicago: Moody, 1994), 43.
2. Branon, 44.
3. Hank Hersch, "Big Man on the Block," *Sports Illustrated,* 1 May 1986, 33.
4. Hersch, 33.
5. Branon, 37.
6. Mark Eaton with Kyle Rote, Jr., "Center of Attention," *Sports Spectrum,* May–June 1991, 18.
7. Eaton, 18.
8. Eaton, 18–19.
9. Eaton, 18–19.
10. Eaton, 18–19.
11. Hersch, 34.
12. Hersch, 34.

☆ Hersey Hawkins ☆

Chapter 3

Height: 6 feet, 3 inches

Weight: 190 pounds

Position: Guard

Birth date:
September 9, 1965

College: Bradley
University

Team:
Charlotte Hornets

Hersey Hawkins: Three-Point Wizard

No one had scored this much since Pete Maravich and Johnny Neumann in the late sixties and early seventies. The guard who was doing it was known as "Hawk" to his friends. He was no "gunner"; he was a three-point shooter who kept his shooting percentage in the high thirties. And could he score!

The first game of his senior year at Bradley, Hersey Hawkins rang up 42 points against New

Orleans. The next game, against Colorado, he raised it a notch: 44 points. Only days later against the University of California at Irvine, he plugged in 51 points. Finally, on February 22, 1988, he inundated the basket with 63 points against the University of Detroit Titans.

As a senior Hersey was the number-one NCAA scorer in the country with 1,125 points and a 36.3-points-per-game average—the seventh-best single season in NCAA history. He was the fifth player in Division I history to score over 3,000 points during his college career.

Suddenly, *Sports Illustrated* and *The Sporting News* came calling. They wanted to do articles on this "hotshot" from Chicago. That year, 1988, he was named College Player of the Year by the Associated Press, United Press International, the United States Basketball Writers Association, and *The Sporting News*. It was a big moment for a kid with a lot of heart.

But it was almost not meant to be. As a freshman in high school, Hersey tried out for the basketball team, but then found out that they had practice in the morning and afternoon. He just didn't want to wake up at 6:00 A.M., play ball, go to school, and play more ball afterwards. It cut twelve hours out of his day.

He quit.

That was when his mother, Laura Hawkins, got involved. She didn't want her boy growing up on the streets, possibly ending up on drugs or a drunk, or even worse, dead. She sat Hersey down and explained everything. Then she told him he couldn't quit again.

Hersey returned to basketball his sophomore year and never looked back. He found out he could play, and soon he was playing regularly for his high school team. At center.

Yes, center. He was six-three, extremely small for center, almost too small for forward. But the team was small. So Hersey learned to defend, block, rebound, pivot, and pick. His coach was a friend of Dick Versace, the renowned college coaching wonder and playmaker at Bradley University in Peoria, Illinois. Dick came down to watch Hersey play one night, and he was impressed. None of the other big schools were calling, so he offered Hersey a scholarship at Bradley.

Hersey didn't need another push. And that was just as well—he might have gotten lost at one of the larger schools. But Bradley was Division I, and it had a respectable history plus a fairly famous coach known for cultivating all-Americans and players with NBA ability.

It was a good fit. Hersey slipped right into the starting five as a freshman guard and was soon averaging 15 points per game. He wasn't setting any records, but he was only a freshman; he wasn't expected to set the world on fire.

During Hersey's sophomore year, he drummed the number up to 19 points a game and learned some new moves, developed his "inside" game, and began a style of play that majored on shooting from outside the three-point line. He led the Bradley Braves to a 31–2 record and the NCAA Tournament. They beat the University of Texas at El Paso in the first game, but lost out to the Louisville Cardinals in the second. It was a quick end to a spectacular season.

Then disaster struck. Dick Versace was accused of recruiting violations, though none had occurred while Hersey was at Bradley. Versace left, and Hersey thought about transferring to Villanova.

The new coach, Stan Albeck, realized he needed to keep Hersey at Bradley. He took the boy aside and assured him he could handle a high scorer like Hersey. He had recently coached the Chicago Bulls, who had Michael Jordan, and he'd worked with high hitters Otis Birdsong and George Gervin. He said in *Sports Illustrated,* "I told him about Ice and Otis and Michael. I promised him we could make him an even better player than he already was."[1] Hersey decided to stay put.

Albeck ran an NBA-style offense that focuses on a key player, who usually becomes the high scorer. The object is to get that player into scoring position and let him shoot. It's an exciting offense to watch and NBA superstars Michael Jordan and Charles Barkley have benefited from it. Under Albeck's leadership, Hersey came through with 27 points a game.

That set the stage for Hersey's exciting, record-setting senior year when he averaged 36.3 points a game and won a multitude of awards and honors. He holds Bradley's all-time scoring record and stands fifth in the NCAA with 3,008 career points, ahead of such scoring whizzes as Oscar Robertson and Danny Manning.

Still, Albeck was not always satisfied with Hersey's performance. He wanted the kid to shoot more, to be more aggressive! "I've got to beg the guy to shoot!"[2] Albeck told *Sports Illustrated.* Against University of North Carolina at Charlotte, Hersey threw Jerry Thomas a pass because he was open, but Thomas ripped Hersey for it. Hersey said, "It was the first time anyone ever told me 'I don't care if I'm in the open! Shoot the ball!'"[3] Hersey was that good and that respected by his teammates.

With his last year at Bradley behind him, Hersey was prime NBA-draft material. The Los Angeles Clippers pulled him in with the sixth pick, and then immediately traded him

45

to the Philadelphia 76ers. It was not the kind of move Hersey could have wanted because Philadelphia already had their star shooter in Charles Barkley, but Hersey found himself becoming friends with Barkley and respecting him. "We never had a problem," he says. "He was one guy who I knew from day one. He sort of took me under his wing when I got here. He was there when I had those 3-for-15 nights. He said it was gonna be all right."[4] In time, Hersey began to flow with the 76ers.

During his first year with the team, Hersey struck up a friendship with the team chaplain, Bruce McDonald. The chaplain talked to Hersey about a relationship with Christ. Hersey wasn't ready then, but he says now, "I remember him talking to me in my rookie year. We went to lunch. He talked about Christ and what was in store for me. He said for me to come to him when I was ready. I didn't think about it much then."[5]

Hersey set the 76ers' record for most points by a rookie. Philadelphia made the playoffs but was shut down in three games by the Knicks, as Hersey shot 3 for 24 from the field. He was discouraged, but he resolved not to let it happen again.

His next year with the 76ers, Hersey chipped in with a 23.5 scoring average in their ten playoff games. Then in 1990–91, he improved his regular-season scoring average to 22.1 points per game. In the playoffs, he rang up 20.9 points a game to keep the 76ers respectable.

It was in 1991–92 that Hersey felt a shift in his attitude. He didn't feel he was playing well, and he wasn't enjoying the games as much. Philadelphia didn't make it to the playoffs, either. He came home to his wife and children grumbling and down. He says, "I wasn't happy going to the gym to practice. The only way to get myself on track . . . to get the bad feelings out of me was to give myself to the Lord. I didn't want to come home and argue with my wife about basketball anymore. It was the best decision in my life."[6]

What exactly happened? Bruce McDonald, the chaplain, continued to have an influence. Hersey says, "Bruce was always there to make sure things were going well with me. He's always seemed to have a sense when things weren't going well. I would receive a letter in the mail from him saying, 'Keep your chin up, and we're praying for you.'"[7]

It was during his fourth season with the 76ers that things came together. Hersey, in a very private way, put his faith in Christ. No one had prodded him; he simply knew he had to do it. Hersey talked about his conversion experience in *Sports Spectrum*:

I had been thinking about it for a couple of months. What if something happened? Would I end up in heaven or hell?

47

My wife [Jennifer] was already a Christian. She never pressured me. Never once. When it happened, she was thrilled as I was. I appreciate her a lot more now. I try to be a lot more understanding. I have a lot better relationship with her and the kids.[8]

Bruce McDonald was especially pleased, and happy that Hersey had made the decision himself, without pressure from his wife or others. And other people began to notice the change in Hersey too. He was quieter, according to Doug Moe, the 76ers' coach. Hersey was leading by exam-ple. Moe called him a "class act."

Armon Gilliam, one of the 76ers' forwards, believes that Hersey was able to refine his abilities, perhaps as a result of his walk with Christ. There was more peace, more stability, more quiet development and growth. He said, "I think when he came into the league, he was more or less a shooter. Now I think he's a versatile scorer. He's pretty tough to guard because of that."[9]

Because of that walk with Christ, Hersey now has a much clearer idea of where basketball fits into his life. He goes out and plays as hard as he can, but it's still a job. Basketball is no longer "everything," as he once felt and lived and believed. Now he takes the time to enjoy his family, nourish and cherish his wife, and guide his children.

McDonald has also noticed another dimension of Hersey's walk with Christ. "They [Hersey and Jennifer] are instigators to get people to Bible studies. He has a boldness to share and a desire to grow as a husband. He's sensitive to help other people in ministry."[10]

Why this boldness? Why this determination to help others? Hersey says, "I want them to realize the feeling I have in knowing there's something better when you leave here. I invite any of my friends who I'm close to. Just coming to chapel and Bible study—it's a start. Maybe they'll think they do need to give their life to the Lord. I want them to know there's a sacrifice, but they'll be rewarded for it. When it's all over, I want them to be in heaven."[11]

The thing that separates Hersey from the pack, besides his faith in Christ, is his dead accuracy at three-point shooting. When he was at Bradley, he hit 35.9 percent of his three-point attempts. In Philadelphia, he increased that number to over 40 percent. In his career, he has canned 476 of 1172 trey (three-point) attempts. That's 40.7 percent, an average ranked as seventh in the all-time NBA statistical records. He also holds the 76ers' single-season record of 108 three-pointers.

How can you become an able three-point shooter? Hersey gives two lines of advice: First, practice until you feel comfortable—"Just like shooting a free throw." And then, when you step onto the court, you have to feel confident you're going to score.[12]

Hersey is happy if he can basket 4 of 10 attempts from the three-point line. But if he reaches 6 for 10, as he did in one eight-game stretch during the 1992–93 season when he went 17 for 28, he's especially happy.

That was an earmark season for Hersey. Barkley had been traded, and now he was captain of the team. He led the team in minutes played and scored 20 or more points 40 times. (He even hit for 40 points in one game and 39 in another.) In the end, he missed only one game. It was a rip-roaring season, and he had proved he was valuable to the team.

But the 76ers had other ideas. They wanted to rebuild, and to do that they knew they'd have to trade away some of their heavy hitters, starting with Hersey Hawkins. On September 3, 1993, Hersey was shipped off to the Charlotte Hornets. Hersey himself didn't flinch at the deal; in fact, he liked it. "I was going somewhere where we had the potential to do something. Going to a younger team. Plus I think they were getting something good. I enjoyed myself in Philadelphia. I think the organization treated me well."[13]

But he keeps his head up with the Hornets. With Philadelphia, Hersey was the go-to guy, and even with Barkley in the starting five, he was number two at worst. But with players like Larry Johnson, Alonzo Mourning, Dell Curry, and Eddie Johnson on the

Hornets, he realized he might be number three or four, or even five. That took some getting used to.

Unfortunately, injuries to Mourning and Johnson held the Hornets back during the 1993–94 season, and it was upsetting. But it did open up the court for Hersey to do his heavy hitting. One night, he even blew in 41 points against the Warriors. He was hanging in there, spinning in those treys and running a potent pick-and-post game.

Above all, Hersey thinks of his commitment to Christ. "I want to bring my family some stability and some peace of mind," he says. "Hopefully they know that I'll always be there for them, and when I go on the road Jennifer doesn't have to worry about me doing anything. She can trust me. With the boys, I want them to be secure that I'm their daddy. They can talk to me. They can have fun with me. I'll be there for them."[13]

He continues to read his Bible as much as he can and to gather around him people who are spiritually sound and committed. He loves Bible study and group discussion and is always open to hearing others' opinions and ideas. He thanks Jesus every morning and night for the strength and ability to play ball. He knows people are watching, and when things are going bad, he wants to be a good example of faith and determination to do right. He's always looking forward to tomorrow.

And to sinking another of those three-pointers!

1. Alexander Wolff, "Scoring in Highest Style," *Sports Illustrated,* 25 January 1988, 25.

2. Wolff, 25.

3. Wolff, 25.

4. Jeff Smith, "The Legacy of Laura Hawkins," *Sports Spectrum,* May–June 1993, 8.

5. Smith, 9.

6. Smith, 9.

7. Dave Branon, *Slam Dunk* (Chicago: Moody, 1994), 106.

8. Smith, 9.

9. Smith, 9.

10. Smith, 9.

11. Smith, 9.

12. Smith, 9.

13. Branon, 108.

14. Branon, 108–9.

☆ **Buck Williams** ☆

Height: 6 feet, 8 inches

Weight: 225 pounds

Position: Forward

Birth date: March 8, 1960

College: University of Maryland

Team: **Portland Trail Blazers**

Chapter 4

Buck Williams: Up for the Rebound

Coming into this world, Charles "Buck" Williams didn't have a lot going for him. His mother picked cotton for four dollars a hundred pounds—on good days, she picked three hundred pounds. When Buck was a baby, his mother often laid him in the bag she threw the bolls into. Sometimes she laid him on a blanket on the ground, but then she had to watch out for the snakes—they'd go right down a baby's throat searching for fresh milk. Fortunately, no snake ever stuck its snout down Buck's throat with his watchful mother nearby.

Growing up in Rocky Mount, North Carolina, was tough. Buck's father worked construction for ten cents a day. One year he managed to build the family a little four-room house, but it was little more than a shack and had no running water or indoor plumbing.

Years later, after becoming a pro basketball player with the New Jersey Nets, one of Buck's proud moments was buying his parents a real "mansion" with four bedrooms, three bathrooms, and plenty of showers! His mom and dad were as proud of Buck as Buck was of them.

His humble beginnings never daunted Buck. In junior high school, he played both football and basketball. He liked football, but his basketball coach kept him out of the football games: He didn't want Buck to get hurt and be unable to play basketball. Buck only played two football games that year before he said good-bye to football and concentrated on basketball.

Buck's junior high and high school coach (his last two years) was a man named Reggie Henderson. Coach Henderson was a strong and excellent influence who became one of Buck's greatest friends and mentors, and remains so today. Buck says, "Everybody talks about having a mentor. Coach

Henderson has been my mentor for a very long time, and I owe a great deal of my success to him. We are best of friends. We talk on the phone, we get together whenever we can, and we have just a very good relationship."[1]

Buck's Rocky Mount team did well his first few years, but his senior year was the highlight. The team won the state championship, and Buck made all-state and averaged 20 points and 20 rebounds a game during the tournament. People were already recognizing that this tall kid from North Carolina was headed for the big time.

It was during those early years that Buck formed the values and belief system he holds today. His parents were both believers and made him attend church every Sunday. Buck also had a friend named Wesley Johnson, whose mother was a stalwart believer. One day she talked to Buck about the need to accept Jesus, and he did.

But it was the church atmosphere that instilled in him the outlook that honors hard work, good morals, and clean living. "Church helped me shape my morals and values," he says. "It was really sort of an extension of what I was being taught at home. When I found myself out in the world, I had a foundation to build on. I knew the sort of direction I had to be headed in."[2]

Buck also gives credit to his personal relationship with Christ:

To have a personal relationship with Jesus Christ has been phenomenal in my life. I often wonder why I make some decisions. Well, it's not me making them, but God is really taking control in my life and sort of steering me in the right direction when it comes time to make decisions. I always tell people who are asking, 'Buck, how can you stay injury-free, and how do you make the decisions that you make' that it's not so much I'm making them, it's just that I'm leaning on God and praying that He can give me the kind of guidance I need.[3]

After a stellar career in high school, Buck accepted a scholarship to the University of Maryland because he wanted to play under the head coach there, Lefty Driesell. His first year as a Terrapin (1978–79), Buck was named Atlantic Coast Conference Rookie of the Year. He led the conference in rebounding and piled up impressive stats in assists and shooting.

In 1980, after his sophomore season, a real dream was in the making: Buck made the U.S. Olympic basketball team. In preparation for the Olympics, the team played a number of NBA teams and did well. Buck's defensive abilities especially made him a standout, and scouts and fans commented that he looked like NBA material.

Buck's hopes of playing Olympic basketball were dashed when, because of the Soviet Union's war in Afghanistan, President Jimmy Carter decided the United States would boycott the Olympics scheduled that summer in Moscow. Even though it was a disappointment, in some ways Buck regarded it as a sign of God working all things for good. He had been able to play the NBA big boys and had gotten some recognition.

Buck returned to Maryland and played out his junior year. He got his name in the record books too. Hitting 64.7 percent of his field goals (183 for 283), he set a school record. He also made second-team all-ACC for the second time. Ultimately, he finished his college career with a 61.5-percent shooting percentage, one of the highest ever.

The Terrapins won 21 games that year and were ranked eighteenth in the country. In the NCAAs they lost their second-round game to Indiana, the ultimate NCAA champion. Buck planned to return to finish out his senior year, but then something he read changed his mind:

> It was sort of interesting. I had no idea I was going to turn hardship and go to the NBA. At the

last minute I happened to read an article in *The Washington Post* and Bob Ferry, who was the GM of the Bullets, stated in the paper that if underclassmen like Buck Williams would decide to leave college, they would probably go in the top five or ten picks.

So that gave me an idea that I might be wanted. I got on the phone and called some people, and after we got some guarantees I decided to come out. It was the best decision, and with the conditions of my family, it was a way I could improve their condition and do some things I wanted to do for them. I missed my senior year of college and the social aspect of it, which you can never regain once you lose it. But later I went back and finished my degree [in 1988], so it was a good decision.[4]

The New Jersey Nets took him in the first round, third pick overall. Buck was in prime position for big play and big money. With the Nets, he began making some long strides and was rookie of the year in 1982. The Nets compiled a 44–38 record and made the playoffs. The next year the Nets had another winning season, 49–33, losing again in the playoffs. Buck was a big part of their success.

In 1984 the Nets compiled 45 wins, but lost in the playoffs again. It was discouraging at the time, but Buck felt their game was looking up. He'd brought the team from consistent losing records to consistent winning records. He had also made all-pro and the all-defensive team, and was considered the mainstay of the team with his fierce rebounding, excellent shooting, and tough defensive presence.

Buck became an expert at using his body to veer his man away from the basket. All that body whopping sends some tempers into the upper decks, but Buck became known as the cool man on the court because he never got into fights, and he kept his temper when others lost theirs. It all goes back to his relationship with Jesus. "If I wasn't a Christian," says Buck, "I doubt if I would respond in the same way. My parents always taught me the right way to handle my anger and pride. Now it comes very naturally. Reading the Bible helps a great deal. I think the Bible outlines clearly how to live your life. I try to live according to Bible standards."[5]

Unfortunately, the next few years in New Jersey were sour with bitter losing seasons. In 1987–88, the Nets won only 19 of their 82 games.

Nonetheless, Buck kept his attitude right and his faith strong. From 1985–89 Buck played in almost all the Nets games, not missing a single game in the earlier seasons. In the 1985–86 season, he scored over 20 points 22 times. In 1986–87, he led the league with 701 defensive rebounds, averaged 18.3 points per game (his highest ever), and was named to the all-defensive second team.

Still, it was hard to keep coming out night after night knowing a loss would be the likely result:

My Christian experience kept my boat anchored during my last three years in New Jersey. I had the privilege of being associated with a church called Redeeming Love Christian Center. And my faith really grew by leaps and bounds. A couple of verses in Romans that talk about how through adversity and hard times I should still be happy (Romans 5:3, 4), helped me get through the whole ordeal. . . .

Everyone would always ask me, "Buck, how can you play so hard when you're not going to win any games?" But through it all, I knew deep in my heart that I was becoming a better person—I was building character. I was also becoming a better basketball player because I was playing on a losing team, which forced me to go out and do more things to help the team.[6]

Lean years come to an end most of the time, and for Buck they ended on June 24, 1989. That was the day he was traded to the Portland Trail Blazers, one of the up-and-comers in the NBA. Buck immediately began making his voice and moves felt on the court. In 1988–89, the Trail Blazers had gone 39–43. That was B.B.: Before Buck. In 1989–90, they jumped to 59–23 and went all the way to the NBA finals against the Pistons. They didn't come away with the championship, but it was a start.

His first year with the Blazers, Buck made the NBA's all-defensive first team. He pulled down 800 rebounds, the best the Blazers had seen in eight years. His defensive ability on the court sliced 6 points off the Blazers' scored-against average, too, and accounted for many of the extra wins.

In 1992, the Trail Blazers returned to the NBA championships, and Buck was right in the middle of it, as he had been that whole season. In fact, the 1991–92 season was one of Buck's best. He led the NBA in field-goal-shooting percentage, with 60.4 percent of his flings hitting pay dirt (340 for 563). He led the Blazers in both defensive and offensive rebounding with 444 and 260, respectively. He averaged 11.3 points a game, with a high of 23.

Portland zoomed into the playoffs, beating the Lakers in round one, 3–1. Then they knocked out Phoenix in the Western Conference semifinals, 4–1. In the Western Conference finals, Portland rolled over the Utah Jazz, 4–2. Buck, along with teammates Clyde Drexler, Terry Porter, Jerome Kersey, and Cliff Robinson, were scoring, picking, screening, and shooting exceptionally well.

Then they ran up against the Chicago Bulls with their amazing man of the airways, Michael Jordan. Though the record doesn't look like it, it was a climactic battle. As always, the Bulls were formidable: They had finished the regular season with the best record in the NBA, and they kicked Portland all over the court the first game, 122–89. It was no contest.

But in the second game, Portland came alive and trashed the Bulls, 115–104.

Then, in a tight defensive contest, Chicago took a second game, 94–84. Once again it was closer than it looked. Portland came back to tie the series at 2–2 with another win, 93–88. Portland was getting its game back, and Michael Jordan had gotten a little quiet.

The final two games were exciting, but only one was close. Chicago won the fifth game handily, 119–106. Then, in a tight defensive and rebounding contest, Portland almost came back to tie the series but Buck and his teammates lost the final game, 97–93.

Despite those two championship losses, Buck Williams keeps his chin up and his faith strong:

> You need Jesus Christ as your focal point. For example, everything else around you changes— like I had to change in my life from New Jersey to Portland. I had another change in my life when I had my son. In other words, as everything around you changes, you keep your focus on the Lord, as the Bible talks about, "seek ye first the kingdom of God . . . and these things will be added to you" (Matthew 6:33).
>
> And that's my way of thinking. Seeking the kingdom of God keeps me focused—which is so important in my life and so important when I walk out on the floor. I need to be focused on what I have to get done while everything else around me

is changing. It could be a change in our defense, or the other team may put in a different player to guard me, or the pace of the game may change. But if I can stay focused on what has to be done in terms of rebounding and playing defense, I will be more consistent, and I will get the reward in the end.[7]

In an article in *Sports Spectrum* magazine, Buck gave some advice about passing that is worth passing on.

In learning to be a good passer in basketball, you also have to be consistent. You have to sort of give up yourself. You don't get the accolades, you don't get the headlines if you become a great passer—unless you are Magic Johnson and you incorporate the other parts of your game. So you really have to be unselfish. You also have to have a court awareness to know where the rest of the players are on the floor. You sort of have to have an eye in the back of your head, always looking to make that pass. I think whatever you do in life, if you're consistent at it, you're going to be pretty good, whether it is rebounding, passing, or shooting. And, of course, it takes a lot of hard work and practice.[8]

Buck Williams is the classic "unselfish" player. He passes so others can get off the shots, sets up screens and picks so others can lay them in, and when they miss, he rebounds—like no one else.

In Buck's own words, his goal is to touch and help others. "I want to touch someone's life," he says. "If I touch one person's life for good, then my own life will not be in vain."[9]

A high and admirable goal for anyone.

1. Dave Branon, *Slam Dunk* (Chicago: Moody, 1994), 254.
2. Branon, 255.
3. Branon, 255.
4. Branon, 257.
5. Bobbie Braker, "Bucking the Trend," *Sports Spectrum,* September–October 1991, 12.
6. Buck Williams with Kyle Rote Jr., "Rebounding in Rip City," *Sports Spectrum,* March–April 1991, 6–8.
7. Williams, 9.
8. Williams, 9.
9. Branon, 261.

Chapter 5

Height: 5 feet, 11 inches

Weight: 175 pounds

Position: Guard

Birth date: March 25, 1965

College: Southern University (Louisiana)

Team: **San Antonio Spurs**

☆ Avery Johnson

Avery Johnson: Mr. Assist

Few people take the route to the NBA that Avery Johnson has taken. He was never drafted. He has always played as a free agent. He has moved quickly from team to team and never put down any real roots.

Still, the man has heart and faith. And that has kept him steady through the ups and downs of an exciting NBA career.

Avery began life in a poor family in New Orleans,

the ninth of ten children. His mother was a home-maker, his father the foreman of a construction crew. From his Christian parents he learned the values of faith, commitment, and hard work. "My father and I had a great relationship. Everything that a father-son relationship should be. He was a hard-working man. And both of my parents always instilled things in terms of hard work, confidence, and those types of values."[1]

Avery has more to say about his father:

> My father taught me everything. He taught me how to be a husband, how to be a father, how to work. He worked sixty years without a vacation. He just taught me about working hard and being the best you can be and putting that extra effort into things. A lot of self-discipline stuff. My dad was not an athlete. He only had a sixth grade education. But he knew stuff about the Lord and just life in general.[2]

It was his home and his relationship with his father that kept Avery from joining a gang and running the streets of New Orleans like so many of his friends. His mother determined that all her children would be in church Sunday morning and night. And through the church's influence, she kept Avery away from drugs and drinking.

But years later, Avery would find himself a "Sunday Christian" in need of redemption. He'd made it into the NBA and could party with the best of them.

Money and women became his "gods." Even though he still went to church, it wasn't his focus. He knew he'd come a long way, but he had a lot farther to go. And he knew he was headed for hell.

But that's getting ahead of things. Let's go back to a little five-foot-three-inch senior in high school. He'd made the varsity, but he was riding the bench—the "pine," as players sometimes call it. He didn't play, and he was frustrated. He was sure he could perform. He knew how to pass, how to assist, and how to score, and he wanted a chance to show his skills.

Even though Avery wasn't yet a Christian, God must have been watching. One of Avery's friends on the team, the starting point guard, was let go—he never knew the reason—and Avery stepped into his position just as the state playoffs were beginning.

Things began to click. Throughout the playoffs, Avery played like an ace, setting up plays, making things happen, getting the ball to teammates who were in position to score—doing everything a point guard is supposed to do. His team finished 35–0 and won the state championship.

Someone else was watching too: a scout from New Mexico Junior College. He noticed the little guy with amazing ball-handling skills and recommended that his school go after Avery. And they did. Avery took a scholarship to New Mexico Junior College, the only college that came calling.

But New Mexico JC was only a stopping place. After a year there, Avery transferred to Cameron University, a Division II school in Lawton, Oklahoma. He was far from great, but even though he only averaged 4.3 points a game, he was learning a lot about playmaking. And he was growing physically, getting close to his final height of five feet eleven inches.

He only stayed one year at Cameron, then shipped off for Southern University, a Division I school. In his junior year, Avery averaged 36 minutes of ball per game for the Jaguars. Since he was the point guard, he did not shoot much, averaging fewer than eight attempts per game.

What he *did* do was pass. During his two years at Southern, he dished out 732 assists in 61 games. That was more assists than all but two *NBA* guards accumulated in the 1992–93 season. And they played 82 games!

Avery led the nation in assists those two years. He says now, "It was definitely a big thrill. It wasn't just leading the conference that I was playing in, but it was the whole nation. So I was out there competing with guys from Duke and Georgetown and all the schools, so it was a great accomplishment."[3]

Avery made the record books too. His 13.3 assists per game in 1987–88 is the best ever for a single season in the NCAA. His career average of 8.9 assists per game also holds the top spot.

Still, Avery knew he had to improve his shooting. He wasn't going to get noticed with a 7.5-points-per-game average even though he did score 21 points in one game against Texas Southern. The same night, he also had 20 assists.

Avery wondered if he had a chance in the NBA. He could definitely make plays—he was the best there was in assists. But was he good enough to play in the big time? He didn't know, but he had to try to find out.

Waiting for the draft is nerve-racking enough for players who know they'll be drafted. But waiting through the whole ordeal and then not getting a bid is sheer agony.

That was what happened to Avery in the 1988 draft. No one came calling.

But that didn't stop this man with a mission. Avery showed up in July at the Seattle Supersonics basketball camp as a free agent. He played his heart out in the summer league in L.A. too, leading in both scoring and assists on a team that included veterans Sedale Threatt, Olden Polynice, Russ Schoene, and Derrick McKey.

Bernie Bickerstaff, the Sonics' coach,

69

noticed Avery's performance. The Sonics already had three point guards—John Lucas, Sedale Threatt, and Nate McMillan—but Avery made the team anyway.

Avery says, "I was playing against guys like Byron Scott [Lakers] and Terry Porter [Blazers], guys that I had been watching on TV. But I held my own. And that really gave Bernie Bickerstaff an idea that I could be a good player down the road."[4]

Unfortunately, being a Sonic was like being back in high school because Avery was "riding the pine" every night. But something else was happening that would play a big role later: Avery was becoming good friends with John Lucas. John was a veteran near the end of his career who was thinking about becoming a coach. Avery and John developed an excellent rapport and John encouraged him. John felt he'd made a lot of mistakes in his NBA career—including being involved in drugs—and he didn't want to see Avery go down the same road. He was there on and off the court for Avery, and Avery responded in kind. He considered John one of his best friends in Seattle.

Even though Avery wasn't seeing much playing time, he was building his skills. His first year he played 291 minutes in 43 games. He had 73 assists and 1.6 points per game. His second year, he came up to 575 minutes in 53 games, almost doubling his playing time. He had 182 assists and averaged 2.6 points per game. He was slowly improving.

It was at this time that Avery made the decision that changed the course of his life. He had been into the party lifestyle of the typical NBA player, spending a lot of money and going around with different women. However, the Bible stories his mother had told him as a kid kept flooding back. He knew something had to change.

"I really took a look at myself," says Avery. "I was at a church service in my hometown of New Orleans where the pastor preached about being fully committed. He talked about people who are just church-goers, people who aren't fully committed, that they're not reaching their fullest potential as Christians. It really just hit me in my heart. I just got up and said, 'I want to change. I want to be a full-time Christian.'"[5]

Soon, Avery was talking to kids in assemblies about his newfound faith. He spoke about Christianity as not being just another religion. It was a relationship with Jesus that involved total obedience.

He was happy. He was sailing. He wasn't playing that much yet, but he was moving up.

Then disaster struck. Another change. The Supersonics traded Avery to Denver. He played in twenty-one games for the Nuggets, and then they let him go—on Christmas Eve, 1990. Avery was out of the NBA and out of a job.

But Avery still believed God knew what he was doing. He believed Jesus would see him through, and he expected that something would come up.

Something did. The San Antonio Spurs drew him in for the rest of the 1990–91 season to fill in for guard John Strickland. But that didn't last either. Twenty games into the 1991–92 season, the Spurs let Avery go. He was without a job once again.

This time Avery found room on the Houston Rockets' roster. He averaged 5.6 points and 3.7 assists per game. At the end of the 1991–92 season, he was a free agent once again.

Six games into the next season, Avery was back with the Spurs on a one-year contract. The Spurs looked like a powerful team that year: They had the two Davids, Robinson and Wood, and things were looking up with their first-year coach, Jerry Tarkanian.

However, 20 games into the season the Spurs were 9–11. Tarkanian complained that he didn't have a point guard, but the boss didn't see it that way. He fired Tarkanian and brought in John Lucas, Avery's old pal in Seattle. John didn't think the Spurs needed a new point guard. They already had one: Avery Johnson.

Suddenly, the Spurs went on a roll. With Avery at point, they won eighteen of their next nineteen games. During that streak, Avery averaged 30.1 minutes, 9.8 points, and 8.6 assists per game. He ended the season with the fourth-highest minutes played on

 the team. He also ranked number four in the league among guards for his assist-and-turnover ratio and averaged 7.5 assists a game. More importantly, the Spurs posted a 49–33 record.

The Spurs opened the playoffs by sweeping the Trail Blazers in four games. The potent Phoenix Suns had to play six games to stop the Spurs in the next round. Avery was riding high.

He says of that season, "Perseverance would definitely describe me, with faith in parentheses. Because I've had to persevere through a lot of different things on and off the court. And I've had to walk by faith and not by sight in a lot of situations."[6]

That faith sustains him and he keeps on going in Christ. He says,

> Our role as Christians is just to serve God. That's why we're here, to serve God and glorify Him and share His light with others. And there are three ways that I stay sharp. I stay on my knees in prayer. I love talking to God. Second, I stay in the Word. I try to read my Bible every day. And third, one of the most important things is staying in the right type of fellowship. I have brothers that I can just talk to and share with. That's really important to me.[7]

One of Avery's big moments as a Christian came in the summer of 1993 when he participated in something the Spurs sponsored called "Jammin' Against the Darkness." David Wood and David Robinson led it.

"When we say, 'jammin' against the darkness,' we basically mean beating the devil," Avery says. "We mean jamming against anything that the devil stands for: drugs, gangs, depression, divorce, racism, sexual immorality. It was a very successful event. We had 800 people give their lives to the Lord the first night and 900 the second night. I've never been a part of anything for the Lord like those two nights. He really used our team. At the time I didn't know if I would be with the Spurs the rest of my career, but I know one thing: God brought me here to be a part of that."[8]

During training camp the next season (1993–94), Avery held out for a higher salary. The Spurs didn't see it his way and released him.

The Golden State Warriors' all-star point man, Tim Hardaway, injured his knee in preseason play. God must have been watching again, because the Warriors called Avery within an hour. As a result, he joined Chris Webber and Latrell Sprewell with the Warriors on October 25, 1993. It was one more change in a career of many changes.

If there is a message Avery has for kids, it's the idea of putting Jesus first:

No matter what you do, just put God first. Be strongly committed to Him, because without Him we are nothing. And I don't want Jesus to think that what He did on the cross was in vain for me. I want to continue to do all that I can while I'm on this journey. That's pretty much what I try to share with kids: putting God first and just striving for excellence.

God sent His best gift in Jesus, so whenever you're in the classroom or whenever you're participating in sports or whatever it is, do it to the best of your ability.[9]

Avery Johnson has seen plenty of changes in his life. Whether or not he remains with Golden State, you can be sure he'll not fade from view. He'll be scoring a little, forcing turnovers, and making those assists. Above all, he'll be serving Jesus.

That's what it's all about!

---

1. Rob Bentz, "The Little Guard That Could," *Sports Spectrum,* November 1993, 18.
2. Dave Branon, *Slam Dunk* (Chicago: Moody, 1994), 117–18.
3. Branon, 119–20.
4. Bentz, 18.
5. Bentz, 19.
6. Bentz, 19.
7. Bentz, 19.
8. Branon, 124–25.
9. Branon, 127.

☆ Craig Ehlo ☆

Chapter 6

Height: 6 feet, 7 inches

Weight: 205 pounds

Position: Guard

Birth date: August 11, 1961

College: Washington State University

Team: **Atlanta Hawks**

Craig Ehlo: Mr. Everything

He's tall for a guard, short for a forward, and he's fast. So sometimes he plays off guard, sometimes point guard, and sometimes small forward—that's how he got the nickname Mr. Everything. A Cleveland TV reporter gave the name to him, and it fits.

In his twelfth season in the NBA, Craig Ehlo is an old man now at age 33. He's hung around longer than the average player. How did he get started in basketball?

Actually, he wanted to play football as a kid, and he could have made a formidable tight end. He grew up in football country—Lubbock, Texas—which definitely made football more appealing. Hardly anyone had heard of the NBA when Craig was growing up. He didn't like football that much, though. He tended to hurt after he got hit, and he was tall and skinny, so he got hit a lot.

Craig's high school basketball coach, Joe Michalka, encouraged him to stick with basketball. Basketball was in his blood too: His mother had played in high school and college—the old six-on-six style.

After a fair career in high school, Ehlo attended Odessa College, a two-year school in the area. He did well, looping in 12 points a game during his freshman year. In 1980–81 his 20 points a game and excellent play caught the eye of several scouts and coaches, some of whom thought he might be NBA material. A lot of colleges began looking at him too, including the formidable University of Texas.

Eventually, though, UT passed and Craig ended up at Washington State University in the far north. It was the land of trees and mountains, very different from his home in Texas. It was a nice change.

At Washington State, Craig played under Coach George Raveling. He settled down to a 12-point average per game and had good rebounding and assist stats. He filled out to the upper 190s, and began to handle the rough and clutch play of the college circuit.

Still, Craig wasn't thinking about the NBA. It never occurred to him to try for it, let alone think someone would be interested. Fortunately, Coach Raveling knew better. He began playing Craig up to several coaches in the NBA and sent him to several basketball camps that summer, including the NBA predraft camp.

The camp Craig attended was a rookie camp with the Houston Rockets. Unfortunately, after a great camp, he tore some ligaments in his ankle. However, the Rockets coach, Bill Fitch, told him he was staying on the team and that, once he healed up, he'd be playing. Craig was lucky: According to the rules, Fitch couldn't release him until he'd healed and been given a full chance.

After surgery and recovery, Craig began playing for the Rockets. He played in only seven games his first year, but in one game against the San Antonio Spurs he scored 14 points, pulled down six rebounds, and made three assists. He had the goods. He could make it in the NBA. During the next summer, he averaged 19 points a game in a minileague. He was on the road again!

But things didn't take off for Craig as he'd hoped. In the next two years he barely played in half the Rockets' games. He scored just 185 points. He was the guy who came in for Hakeem Olajuwon or Ralph

Sampson after they'd finished their 30- or 40-point stints; that is, when it was all over—when the game was in the bag.

The Rockets lost in the finals to the Boston Celtics that year. In the final game, the Rockets found themselves 19 points behind with six seconds to go. With fans pouring onto the court, Craig drove to the basket and made the final shot, a lay-up. It was to be his last point with the Rockets. He was waived on October 30, 1986.

Unemployment for anyone is not a happy condition, but for an NBA player it's especially terrifying. You can't easily go calling yourself—not when the season is just about to start. You have to wait for the call from another team. Craig's agent advised him to wait for the call, which he did.

But no one called.

No one except for the Continental Basketball Association, a minor league not connected to the NBA. A friend of his was a coach and wanted Craig to play for him. So Craig played for the Mississippi Coast Jets. Have you heard of them? Neither have most of us. But Craig put in his time. He played in six games, and suddenly the Cleveland Cavaliers came around. Mark Price, their all-star guard, had appendicitis. They needed someone to fill in. Craig's name was mentioned. Would he consider?

You bet! Craig signed a ten-day contract.

Note that: ten days. Not an unusual thing in the NBA. Plenty of players have signed those kinds of contracts just to get a foot in the door. It often happens when a star player is injured and a team suddenly needs someone not on their present roster to fill in.

It was a life-changing moment. Craig played well for Price. He signed on with the Cavaliers for the rest of the year.

Then Cavaliers guard John Bagley suffered an injury. Craig immediately had a chance to play full time! He did especially well in one five-game stretch, averaging 15.4 points, 8.4 rebounds, and 5.6 assists for that period. Then, two weeks after putting on Cavalier colors, he bumped up the pace and shot in 26 points against Atlanta. In his first year with the Cavs he ended up scoring more points (in 44 games) than during his whole time in Houston. He was rolling.

Eventually, Mark Price came back into the lineup and Craig went back to backup. But a friendship began. Craig had heard about Mark and his so-called Christian testimony. He even called Mark "choir boy" on several occasions. But Mark didn't react negatively to the ribbing.

Craig was at a crossroads in his spiritual life at that time. He didn't know exactly what he believed about a relationship with Jesus. He had gone forward at a Billy Graham Crusade in Lubbock when he was thirteen but he began to realize he'd probably only done it to please his friends. Though he attended church, he didn't understand much of what he read in the Bible, which he rarely studied.

Mark and Craig became such good friends that they began doing everything together. They even purchased houses across the street from one another. They went to practice together, rode in the same car to the airport for away games, and played in the gym that summer. Craig thought Mark would be talking about God constantly, but he didn't. Craig relates his greatest spiritual moment this way:

> Then one night in November of 1987 we were over at his house with his aunt and his wife. We were just having the old cakes and cookies and talking, and I guess he felt it was on his heart to ask me if I was going to heaven if I died. . . .
>
> Any other time I would have beat around the bush when someone asked me that, but this time when he asked me I said, "No, I don't know Jesus. I don't know what it takes." I gave him a confident

answer, and he gave me a confident answer back.

After that, we discussed some things about how and why God wants me to be in His kingdom. And I accepted Jesus as my personal Savior that night.[1]

Craig's greatest professional moment was yet to come. In a playoff game against the Chicago Bulls on May 7, 1989, Craig was at the top of his form. He'd played in every game of the season and helped the Cavaliers tie the Lakers for the second-best win-loss record in the NBA. His stats were his best ever.

It was the first round of the Eastern Conference playoffs, and the Cavaliers were hungry. They had lost to Chicago the previous year and now they wanted a win.

With only seconds remaining in the game, behind by a point, the Cavs brought the ball up and passed it around. The seconds were ticking away. Just a little bit of time left. Who would put in the last points? Mark Price? Ron Harper? Both were scoring well.

No, it was Craig Ehlo. Driving the lane, Ehlo stuck a lay-up.

Cavs ahead by one point. Three seconds to go. The crowd went wild.

There was only one person to stop: Michael Jordan. And Ehlo was covering him. He says, "The Bulls set [Jordan] up at the top of the key, and he was just standing there. Larry Nance and I were double-teaming him, but we weren't real tight on him. We gave him enough room to maneuver, and when the play actually started, he just kind of stood there. I thought he was just basically going to be a decoy. But then 'Bam!' he went to the sidelines, caught the ball, took one or two dribbles to the middle, and before you know it, he had a shot going up. I just tried to run in front of him and get a hand up. I was hoping to change the shot a little bit, which I did. But he still had a good shot at the basket, and it went in."[2]

The horn sounded and the game was over! 101–100. The Bulls had won.

When the Cavaliers decided to make some changes after the 1993 season, Craig was let go. He tried free agency. When his old coach at Cleveland, Lenny Wilkins, went to Atlanta, Craig followed.

For someone who never set his sights on the NBA, Craig Ehlo has done pretty well for himself. He's playing the game he loves and serving Jesus Christ. What better combination can you get?

---

1. Dave Branon, *Slam Dunk* (Chicago: Moody, 1994), 60.

2. Branon, 52.

☆ **Mark Price** ☆

Chapter 7

Height: 6 feet

Weight: 170 pounds

Position: Guard

Birth date: February 15, 1964

College: Georgia Tech University

Team: **Cleveland Cavaliers**

Mark Price: Point Man

This all-star point guard for the Cleveland Cavaliers is first and foremost a Christian—he's led several teammates to Christ. For instance, friend and teammate Craig Ehlo became a Christian through his witness. But Mark Price also plays basketball very well. And that's a tough combination to beat in the NBA. People respect Mark's message because they respect the man. And Mark carries the potent message of the gospel everywhere he goes.

Mark comes from a basketball-playing family. His

father, Denny Price, has coached in the NBA and is presently the head coach at Phillips University in Enid, Oklahoma, where Mark grew up. Mark's brother Brent played for the University of Oklahoma and was drafted by the Washington Bullets a couple years ago. And Mark's other brother, Matt, was a standout at Phillips, playing under their father's lead.

The Prices attended church every Sunday. Mark's parents communicated the values of faith, goodness, righteousness, and love daily in their home. They even formed a musical quartet at one point: the three boys and Dad, with Mom on the piano. Many evenings were sung away in that home. Today, Mark has a band called Life Line that cut a gospel album several years ago.

After several stellar high-school seasons, Mark received word from Georgia Tech that he was their man. In fact, Tech's scouts came out seventeen times to see Mark play at Enid. Mark made all-state his senior year and was an all-American. That caused Bobby Cremins, the Georgia Tech coach, to put tremendous confidence in Mark as a playmaker and basketball quarterback at point guard.

The Yellow Jackets had come off a 4–23 year. They were not a formidable team, but they played in the Atlantic Coast Conference (ACC), the nation's toughest Division I conference. Mark was small—just six feet tall—and skinny at under 150 pounds.

Even in college that's small, so you can imagine what it is in the NBA.

While at Georgia Tech, Mark played in the NCAA Tournament (though Tech didn't win it during his four years) and the NIT. In 1983 he was the league's top-scoring freshman, and he finished his four years as the tenth-leading scorer in the history of the ACC. He was an all-American his last three years, and was even named MVP of the ACC Tournament in 1985. That year, Georgia Tech won its first-ever conference title but missed going to the Final Four by losing to Georgetown. A special issue of *Sports Illustrated* featured Mark on the cover with two other college sports people.

In 1986, Mark was drafted in the second round by the Dallas Mavericks, twenty-fifth pick overall. Though many expected him to go in the first round, Mark wasn't fazed by his low selection. His faith told him to be patient and all good things would come to him from God. The Mavericks quickly traded Mark to the Cleveland Cavaliers for a future draft pick. Mark's career was on its way.

How did Mark begin on the path of faith? "My commitment to Christ didn't start until my senior year in high school," he says. "I was at a youth revival at my church when I knew it was my time to give my whole life to Christ. Since that time, my life hasn't been easy, but He's always there to bring me through when it's tough. Even when things are going great, I have to give Him the credit."[1]

He especially gives his dad the credit for nurturing his faith:

> My dad is one person I've admired my whole life more than anybody else—seeing his consistency in his faith through the difficult times as well as the good times. He's been consistent, and he's never wavered.
>
> I think all of us sometimes try to hide behind what our parents believe and think that's what counts for us. I grew up in a Christian home and went to church all of the time, but it wasn't until I was 17 that I really made the decision to trust Christ as my Lord and Savior.[2]

Mark's testimony has sometimes brought strong reaction from other players. But the amazing thing is how many speak highly of him as a man of character who lives up to what he believes. Cavaliers' center Brad Daugherty says, "Mark's a good family guy. He's really quiet, but he works hard and tries to do all the right things. He's just a very good person."[3] Or listen to Craig Ehlo: "I really appreciate the way Mark does things both on the court and off the court. His lifestyle rubs off on a lot of these guys."[4] Finally, Tom Petersburg, the Cavs' chapel leader says, "Mark is one who gives credibility to the gospel, that it actually works in a man's life. It shows up in his character. His lifestyle just backs up what he believes."[5]

Mark himself says, "I just try to be consistent every day and show guys that what I believe in is real, not just a passing fancy. Christ is the cornerstone of my life and everything I do revolves around Him."[6]

Playing for the Cavaliers has been a high point of Mark's life. How important is he to the Cavs? Consider this: sixteen games into the 1990–91 season, Mark tore a ligament in his left knee. After an operation, he was out for the season. The Cavs won two of their next 20 games and finished the season with a 33–49 record.

Mark recovered and was back in gear for the next season. As point guard, he led the team to a 57–25 record. What a change! All because of one player. Makes you think of the old Benjamin Franklin story: "For want of a nail, a shoe was lost; for want of a shoe, a horse was lost; for want of a horse, a soldier was lost; for want of a soldier a battle was lost; for want of a battle, a war was lost!"

Mark has made the all-NBA first team once, and third team twice. He's been an all-star two times. In the 1993 NBA All-Star Game, he scored 19 points, second best on the team behind Michael Jordan, who had 30. He also had four assists and one rebound, playing 23 minutes.

Mark holds the record for the highest free-throw percentage in the playoffs, making 157 of 167 attempts for 94.0 percent. He also has the highest percentage in regular-season play: 1,497 for 1,648, or 90.4 percent.

When it comes to three-point field goals, Price is a master. He's on the list for the most three-point field goals in the playoffs with 50. He's also on the career lists for most three-point field goals attempted (1,410) and made (581), and has one of the highest percentages (.412, fourth on the list). He's sixth on the list for 1992–93, with a .416 percentage.

In points scored, Mark's also up there. His career points-per-game average is 15.9. He averaged 18.2 points per game (the second highest on the team) during the 1992–93 regular season, with a high game of 39. He had 602 assists, the highest on the team.

All those stats point to star material. And yet Mark Price remains quiet, soft-spoken, humble. It all goes back to his relationship with Jesus. "Winning in the ACC, being the MVP in the ACC, and playing in the NBA are things few people attain or even have a chance to try for. The feelings that came along with those events were just great. But I can honestly say that none of it compares to having a personal relationship with Jesus Christ."[7]

He remains one of the best players in the business, and ranks at the top of the free-throw shooters.

What is his advice to those who would learn to shoot free throws well?

1. Use repetition. Find a routine on the line and stick with it. Whether it's three dribbles each time or one, find a routine that you're comfortable with and repeat it each time you're at the line.

2. Keep your elbow in. Don't let your elbow "fly" out. Keep the elbow in and underneath the ball.

3. Look at your target. Be sure to focus on the basket. A look-away pass looks nice, but a look-away shot looks like a miss.

4. Follow through on your shot. Be sure your wrist is bent toward the basket after you've released the ball.[8]

Above all, Mark says, "To be a good basketball player, you have to be committed to doing the best you can. You must start with the fundamentals—dribbling, shooting, passing, and defense—and practice more than you want to. I remember that on Friday nights as a young person, when all my friends were getting ready to go out and have fun, I was getting ready to have my fun down at the gym. I wasn't forcing myself to play, but I just loved basketball and couldn't get enough of it. I think that's the key. If you love basketball and really enjoy playing it and if you keep it in the right place behind your relationship with God, your family, and your studies, you'll become the best basketball player you can possibly be."[9]

All that makes for a power player on the court, in the home, and in the kingdom. Mark Price will continue to lead a team wherever he is, you can be sure of that. And you can be sure the Lord will be with him too.

---

1. Bill Alexson, *Reaching for the Rim* (Nashville: Nelson, 1990), 105.
2. Rob Bentz, "The Mark of a Champion," *Sports Spectrum,* January–February 1993, 8.
3. Bentz, 8.
4. Bentz, 8.
5. Bentz, 8.
6. Bentz, 8.
7. Alexson, 105.
8. Bentz, 9.
9. Alexson, 106.